# BABIES AT THE ZOO

## 3 Jaguar Cubs

### Susan H. Gray

CHERRY LAKE PRESS

Published in the United States of America by
Cherry Lake Publishing
2395 South Huron Parkway, Suite 200, Ann Arbor, MI 48104
www.cherrylakepublishing.com

Content Advisor: Dominique A. Didier, Professor of Biology, Millersville University
Reading Advisor: Marla Conn, MS, Ed, Literacy specialist, Read-Ability, Inc.

Photo credits: ©Digitech Sky/Shutterstock.com, front cover; ©PARFENOV1976/
Shutterstock.com, 1, 2; ©Sumbulistan//Shutterstock.com, 4; ©apple2499/
Shutterstock.com, 6; ©designerhuts/Shutterstock.com, 8; ©Kris Wiktor/
Shutterstock.com, 10, 20; ©Kachalkina Veronika/Shutterstock.com, 12;
©Luigi Petro/Dreamstime.com, 14; ©AndreAnita/Shutterstock.com, 16;
©BaLL LunLa/Shutterstock.com, 18

Library of Congress Cataloging-in-Publication Data

Names: Gray, Susan Heinrichs, author.
Title: Jaguar cubs / written by Susan H. Gray.
Description: Ann Arbor, Michigan : Cherry Lake Publishing, 2020. |
    Series: Babies at the zoo | Includes index. | Audience: Grades K-1.
Summary: "Read about cute jaguar cubs and how zookeepers take care of
    them. This level 3 guided reader book includes intriguing facts and adorable
    photos. Students will develop word recognition and reading skills while
    learning about how these baby animals learn and grow, what they eat,
    and how they socialize with each other. Book includes table of contents,
    glossary, index, author biographies, sidebars, and word list for home and
    school connection"—Provided by publisher.
Identifiers: LCCN 2019034141 (print) | LCCN 2019034142 (ebook) |
    ISBN 9781534158948 (hardcover) | ISBN 9781534161245 (paperback) |
    ISBN 9781534160095 (pdf) | ISBN 9781534162396 (ebook)
Subjects: LCSH: Jaguar—Infancy—Juvenile literature. | Zoo animals—
    Infancy—Juvenile literature.
Classification: LCC QL737.C23 G717 2020 (print) | LCC QL737.C23 (ebook) |
    DDC 599.75/51392—dc23
LC record available at https://lccn.loc.gov/2019034141
LC ebook record available at https://lccn.loc.gov/2019034142

Cherry Lake Publishing would like to acknowledge the work of the Partnership
for 21st Century Learning, a Network of Battelle for Kids. Please visit
http://www.battelleforkids.org/networks/p21 for more information.

Printed in the United States of America
Corporate Graphics

# Table of Contents

## About the Author

Susan H. Gray has a master's degree in zoology. She has written more than 150 reference books for children and especially loves writing about animals. Susan lives in Cabot, Arkansas, with her husband, Michael, and many pets.

Can you name another wild animal similar to a jaguar?

# Great Hunters

Jaguars are powerful, wild cats. They live in Central America and South America. Some jaguars live in zoos.

These cats are **predators**. They hunt all kinds of animals. Jaguars can catch birds. They pounce on **peccaries**. They even eat fish!

Jaguars usually have one or two **cubs** at a time. **Newborns** are helpless. They weigh about 2 pounds (1 kilogram). Their legs are weak. Their little eyes are closed.

Cubs **snuggle** up with their mom. They drink her milk. She licks them clean.

# Zoo Jobs

**Zookeepers** and zoo doctors look after these cats. They give jaguars shots to keep them healthy. They **treat** them for fleas. They even clean their teeth!

Which of your toys do you think a jaguar would like?

Jaguars should not get bored or lazy. So zookeepers let them play with balls and tires. Zookeepers also put out big logs. Jaguars use them to sharpen their claws.

# Learning from Mom

A lot happens in a cub's first 2 months. It gains up to 11 pounds (5 kilograms). It grows strong **muscles**. And it begins to follow its mother around.

The mother jaguar teaches her cubs to hunt. She shows them how to climb trees. She even gives them swimming lessons.

Jaguars stay with their mothers for about 2 years. Then it is time to have their own babies.

New little cubs for mom to snuggle!

# Find Out More

### BOOK
Guillain, Charlotte. *Jaguars.* Chicago, IL: Heinemann Library, 2014.

### WEBSITE
San Diego Zoo Kids—Jaguar
*https://kids.sandiegozoo.org/animals/jaguar*
Learn about jaguars' hunting skills and black jaguars at this site.

# Glossary

**cubs** (KUBZ) the young of some animals, including jaguars

**muscles** (MUHS-uhlz) tissues that move different parts of your body

**newborns** (NOO-bornz) animals that were born recently

**peccaries** (PEK-uh-reez) wild animals related to pigs

**predators** (PRED-uh-turz) animals that hunt and eat other animals

**snuggle** (SNUHG-uhl) to stay close to keep warm or safe

**treat** (TREET) to take care of the health of a person or animal

**zookeepers** (ZOO-kee-purz) people who take care of zoo animals

# Home and School Connection

Use this list of words from the book to help your child become a better reader. Word games and writing activities can help beginning readers reinforce literacy skills.

| | | | | | |
|---|---|---|---|---|---|
| a | clean | healthy | little | pounds | they |
| about | climb | helpless | live | powerful | think |
| after | closed | her | logs | predators | time |
| all | cubs | how | look | put | tires |
| also | do | hunt | lot | sharpen | to |
| America | doctors | hunters | milk | she | toys |
| and | drink | in | mom | shots | treat |
| animal | eat | is | months | should | trees |
| animals | even | it | mother | shows | two |
| another | eyes | its | mothers | similar | up |
| are | first | jaguar | muscles | snuggle | use |
| around | fish | jaguars | name | so | usually |
| at | fleas | jobs | new | some | weak |
| babies | follow | keep | newborns | south | weigh |
| balls | for | kilogram | not | stay | which |
| begins | from | kilograms | of | strong | wild |
| big | gains | kinds | on | swimming | with |
| birds | get | lazy | one | teaches | would |
| bored | give | learning | or | teeth | years |
| can | gives | legs | out | the | you |
| catch | great | lessons | own | their | your |
| cats | grows | let | peccaries | them | zoo |
| central | happens | licks | play | then | zookeepers |
| claws | have | like | pounce | these | zoos |

23

# Fast Facts

**Habitat:** Dense tropical forests

**Range:** Central and South America, Mexico, and possibly Arizona and New Mexico

**Average Length:** From nose to tip of tail, 8 feet (2.5 meters)

**Average Weight:** 100 to 250 pounds (45 to 113 kilograms)

**Life Span:** 12 to 20 years

**Anatomy:** Some jaguars appear to be solid black, but they aren't. They actually have black spots that are darker. The spots can only be seen in bright light.

**Behavior:** Jaguars are good swimmers and do not avoid water.

# Index